# Reflections of the Soul

# Reflections of the Soul

## Christian Poetry

### Book Three of the Heart and Soul Christian Poetry Collection

Esselle Davis

Reflections of the Soul
Christian Poetry
Book Three of the Heart and Soul Christian Poetry Collection
First Edition
ISBN: 9798685769442
© 2020 Esselle Davis
**All rights reserved**

# DEDICATION

Reflections of the Soul
Christian Poetry
is dedicated to:

My husband Tony
My daughter Mandy
The memory of my Mama, Mary
The memory of my Daddy, Doyle

# PREFACE

My journey to writing poetry began when I wanted to send an online greeting to a friend of mine. I couldn't find anything that I liked, or anything that had the message I wanted to send to her. I had a thought to write my own and I thought about what I wanted to say. I wanted it to be something about an angel, so I looked at many images of angels and I finally found one. Looking at that particular picture gave me the thoughts that eventually became a poem. I had managed to write one poem and tried my hand at writing a few more. After receiving encouragement from family and friends I continued to write. There have been times I moved away from writing, but I always come back to it. I find peace in writing and enjoy my time spent writing.

14 And as Moses lifted up the serpent in the wilderness, even so must the Son of man be lifted up:
15 That whosoever believeth in him should not perish, but have eternal life.
16 For God so loved the world, that he gave his only begotten Son, that whosoever believeth in him should not perish, but have everlasting life.
17 For God sent not his Son into the world to condemn the world; but that the world through him might be saved.

John 3:16 King James Version

# Contents

# MAY YOU

May you wake each morning
With a smile on your face
Knowing you are covered
By God's amazing grace

May you have days filled
With happiness and love
And many sweet blessings
Sent from God up above

May you find each afternoon
Filled with a gentle peace
Knowing God's love for you
Will never cease

May you meet each evening
Knowing your day was well spent
May your heart be filled with joy
And your spirit content

May you have nights filled
With needed sleep and rest
Knowing that by the Lord
You are truly blessed

# JESUS IS KNOCKING

If Jesus is knocking
At your heart's door
If to you
He does implore

To open your heart
And let Him in
So He can save your soul
And give you peace within

Answer the call
Then you will see
That from your sins
Jesus can set you free

Jesus will not linger
At your heart's door forever
Make your choice
It could be now or never

If upon the sea of sin
Your soul is rocking
Open your heart while
Jesus is knocking

# WHEN I GET TO HEAVEN

When I get to Heaven
I will view
Many glorious things
All will be new

When I get to Heaven
I will behold
The beautiful streets
Paved with gold

When I get to Heaven
The treasures will unfurl
I will see the
Gates made of pearl

When I get to Heaven
I will see loved ones gone on before
Never to be separated
From them anymore

When I get to Heaven
I will meet Jesus who gave His life for me
I will bow down and thank Him
Because He set me free

# TOGETHER IN HEAVEN

My mother and father
Have both passed away
They each became a flower
In the Master's bouquet

They left this earth
Almost three years apart
Together in Heaven
From Jesus they will never depart

As they each crossed over
Death's chilly sea
They arrived in Heaven
To live happy and free

Even though they can walk
Upon the golden street
I believe they are still
Worshiping at the Savior's feet

They are showing Jesus
Their appreciation
For His shed blood and
Their eternal salvation

# EACH DAY

Each day
As you go along
May you have enough faith
To keep you strong

Each day
As with troubles you do cope
May God fill your spirit
With unending hope

Each day
As you pray to the Father above
May He wrap you in
His pure sweet love

Each day
As life you embrace
May you always know
God's amazing grace

Each day
As you begin anew
May God's loving mercy
Be with you

# SWEET PEACE

Lord there are times
When things go awry
It seems I can't get it right
No matter how I try

When it seems I have reached
The end of my rope
As long as You're there
I still have hope

I talk to you
In earnest prayer
You are a friend
Who truly does care

You listen and hear
My heartfelt plea
Then You send a sweet peace
That comforts me

Dear Jesus I thank you
For this sweet peace
I know your love for me
Will never cease

# NEVER WALK ALONE

When earthly friends forsake me
When they have cast me aside
I feel I have no one
To walk by my side

These times are heartbreaking
I am filled with dismay
But if I stop and think
I can add brightness to my day

Jesus promised He would
Be with me until the end
He always will be
My dearest friend

I seek and I find
Jesus ever so near
He lifts my spirit
He gives my heart cheer

So as I journey into
Life's daily unknown
With Jesus by my side
I will never walk alone

# SITTING AT HIS FEET

If death takes me away
And leaves you here behind
I hope these thoughts
Will bring peace to your mind

I will be in Heaven
So beautiful and fair
There is nothing here on earth
That will ever compare

I will view gates of pearl
I will walk on streets of gold
I will see walls made of jasper
Many other sights I will behold

All of these things
Will bring joy to my soul
As I make my way
Along my Heavenly stroll

I will walk along
The clear crystal sea
But the most precious thing
Is meeting the one who died for me

So when you get to Heaven

As you journey around

Please don't worry

If I can't be found


For I too will be there

In Heaven so sweet

You can find me with Jesus

Sitting at His feet

# A CROWN OF THORNS

A crown of thorns was placed
On the Saviors head
He was hanged on a cross
And suffered and bled

Jesus could have called angels
To get Him down
But he stayed on the cross
And wore the thorny crown

His side was pierced
His body filled with pain
But He accepted His fate
And did not complain

When He came here He knew
He would suffer pain and sorrow
But He came anyway
To give mankind hope for tomorrow

Jesus hanged on the cross
To pay for our sin
Accept Him as Savior
Eternal life you will win

Then one day you will go

To Heaven so fair

To live forever

With Jesus there

When I think of the unsaved

My heart mourns

And I pray they will accept Jesus

Who wore a crown of thorns

# MY LIFEGUARD WALKS ON WATER

My lifeguard walks on water
Waves of life I do not fear
For Jesus is my lifeguard
He always lingers near

Every day is a new chance
To navigate life's sea
Sometimes the waves come
They seek to destroy me

Waves they toss and turn me
Sometimes they knock me down
I sink below the surface
I wonder will I drown

Just below the surface
Then I rise and gasp for air
I have no need to worry
Jesus is already there

Waves of life had covered me
I called out, my Savior came
To safety Jesus pulled me
When I called upon His name

Life's sea may try to drown me

Lead me to my slaughter

But, of sinking I have no fear

My lifeguard walks on water

# WHEN IT BEGINS WITH YOU

Lord, I awoke this morning
I had so much on my mind
I needed to keep moving
I could not get behind

Lord, please understand
I had so much to do
I didn't have five minutes
To spend talking to You

"How did my day go?"
Lord, it's funny that You, ask
Nothing went correctly
It seemed I failed at every task

Lord, I hear You saying
"I would have been there
All You needed to do was
Talk to Me in prayer"

Lord, please forgive me
For pushing You aside
I truly needed You
Today, my steps to guide

I should have began this morning
Upon a bended knee
Lord, asking for Your guidance
In an  humble plea

Lord, when tomorrow comes
And I begin my day
Lord, I will remember
I need to take time to pray

My day may have hardships
I may even end up blue
But, my day is always better, Lord
When it begins with You

# HAPPY NEW YEAR IN HEAVEN

Happy New Year in Heaven
I try to imagine the beauty you see
Still there are times
I wish you were here with me

I wonder if you are walking
Upon the street of gold
Or sitting by the crystal sea
Never growing old

Are you strolling through Heaven
Loved ones there to meet
Or are you all gathered
At the Savior's feet

For me time is measured
In minutes, hours and days
For you time means nothing
It is forever, always

By troubles and trials
You are no longer confined
Knowing you are happy
Brings me peace of mind

Still there are times

I get a little sad

Thinking of you everyday

I miss you Mom and Dad

# I LOVE MY PRECIOUS SAVIOR

I love my precious Savior
He is a friend that is true
If I did not know Him
My life would be so blue

Jesus gave His precious life
To save a sinful wretch like me
He bled and suffered and then died
On the cross of Calvary

He was placed in tomb
And there His body lay
Three days later He rose from the dead
That is what the Scriptures say

He ascended to be with God
In beautiful Heaven up above
He served His earthly mission
With a pure compassionate love

One day I will see face to face
Jesus who saved my soul
I will be with Him in Heaven
The golden streets I will stroll

As I stroll through Heaven
I will view this beautiful place
I will be with my precious Savior
Who saved me by God's grace

The peace and beauty of Heaven
I will enjoy forever more
I will spend eternity with
My precious Savior whom I adore

# THE LAMB

The Sabbath was approaching
Passover was drawing nigh
A sacrifice must be made
A Lamb soon would die

The Lamb had been chosen
His blood soon would spill
He would hang on a cross
He would die on Calvary's Hill

The Lamb was beaten and spat upon
The Lamb they did mistreat
Nailed to a wooden cross
Spikes through His hands and feet

The crowd mocked and cursed Him
The Lamb hanged in despair
Only a few in the crowd
Even seemed to care

The precious Lamb gave His life
Salvation to provide
Blood and water freely flowed
As the soldier pierced His side

On the cross the Lamb suffered

A crown of thorns upon His head

There the Lamb hanged in shame

There His blood was shed


The Lamb's name was Jesus

God's only begotten Son

The world needed a sacrifice

Jesus was the One


It is finished, Jesus cried out in pain

The ground, His blood did stain

The sacrifice had now been made

The Lamb of God was slain

# MY SALVATION IS SURE

Dear Jesus I'm so glad
In You I believe
Thank You for the gift of eternal life
I did receive

By accepting You as Savior
And trusting in Your name
Your wonderful gift
I was able to claim

You are a friend
Faithful and true
You are there each day
To guide me through

Thank You for the blessings
That You send
I know You will be with me
When my life does end

When my time comes
To cross death's chilly sea
You will be there
Waiting for me

You will be there waiting
With arms open wide
Saying my child
You will live now by my side

You will take me to Heaven
My new home
To live with You forever
Nevermore to roam

So even though
Troubles I might endure
Sweet Jesus, my Savior in You
My salvation is sure

# JOY COMES IN THE MORNING

Nothing is perfect
Troubles sometimes come my way
But I can talk to Jesus
Anytime of day

I go to Him
In earnest prayer
He knows my needs
And He does care

The day may be filled
With troubles and sorrow
But when I talk to Jesus
I gain sweet hope for tomorrow

I pray to Him
He hears my plea
Jesus then carries
My burdens for me

Then when I settle in
For my nightly rest
I sleep peacefully
Knowing I am truly blessed

I have learned
During my life
There will be heartaches
There will be strife

But with Jesus in my life
I get peace of mind
Happiness and delight
In Him I can find

Because troubles and trials
May come without warning
But with Christ by my side
Joy comes, in the morning

# I HAVE HOPE

Dear Lord before I met You
My soul was sad and blue
Everyday I wondered
Just how would I get through

It seemed
My sorrow would never end
But You gave me salvation
And became my greatest friend

I still face sickness
And hard times may come to me
But You give me comfort
And will be there to guide me

Lord at times
It may seem all is lost
But I will remember
For my sins You paid the cost

I feel Your love
As You shower me with grace
A smile now replaces
The frown on my face

By Your wonderful love
I am still astounded
My faith in You
Is firmly grounded

I know You are with me
Each and every day
To help me handle
Whatever comes my way

Even when it seems
I'm at the end of my rope
I know You are with me
And I have hope

# GOD'S ANGEL

This is one of God's angels
She's tried and she's true
She's sent to bring blessings
From heaven to you

She will guide you during the times
That you feel lost
She will brace you when
Your ship of life seems tossed

She will be the anchor
That keeps you steady
Day or night
She is always ready

No matter what troubles
Life your way brings
You can find comfort and shelter
Wrapped in her wings

When you have sorrow
She will dry your tears
When you are scared
She will calm your fears

When your are falling
From life's strong demands
She will be there to catch you
In her gentle hands

She will be with you
Through thick and through thin
She will watch over and protect you
All the way to the end

Remember she is sent
From the Father above
To shower you always
With His precious love

# GOD'S LOVE

One day God looked down
On the earth here below
He was saddened at how sin
Continued to grow

The world then needed
A supreme sacrifice
Because nothing that was here
Seemed to suffice

So God sent His Son
Here to die for all sin
Now by believing in Him
The glory you win

Jesus can help
To keep you steady and strong
And close to the Father
Where you belong

Jesus will guide you
Through the day and the night
He's here to lead you
Into the light

That will shine upon you
From God's loving face
For thou art saved
By God's caring grace

Jesus is coming
Back here one day
That's when God's children
Will be going away

To live with the Father
In the new home above
And bask forever
In His unending love

# JESUS IS MY LIGHTHOUSE

When my boat of life
Has drifted far from the shore
When I feel like I can't
Go on anymore

When it seems
I've lost my way
When there is
Darkness in my day

When the fog of despair
Rolls in
When I am upset
And find no peace within

When the rocks of sin
Around me do loom
When the waves roll high and
It seems my boat the sea will consume

When I realize I can't
Handle these problems on my own
When it seems that I am
Completely all alone

Then I look in the direction
Where the shore should be
And I see a bright light
There to guide me

A safe passage now
Comes into my view
I know this storm
I will now get through

The lighthouse is there
Shining it's light
It is guiding me to the shore
With a light so bright

I reach the shore
Safe and secure
This storm of life
I did endure

I look to the lighthouse
That has just led me though
And I see Jesus standing there
Saying I am always here for you

I know I did not make it

Through this storm alone
The light from my Savior
Led me through the unknown

I am now safe in
My Saviors loving care
No matter how dark it seems
His light is always there

# THE MANGER

When God needed to send His Son
To live on this earth
He sent an angel to Mary
To prepare her for His child's birth

She would be the mother
Of God's only Son
The world needed a Savior
And Jesus was the one

Mary was promised to Joseph
They were soon to marry
When he found she was with child
He became wary

Then an angel appeared
To Joseph in a dream
And told him the child
Was the Son of God supreme

Joseph and Mary traveled to Bethlehem
To pay their tax
The journey was long
And Mary needed to relax

They sought for a room
At the local inn
The pains of childbirth
For Mary, were soon to begin

There were no rooms
At the inn to be found
So they sought shelter
In a stable with animals all around

When the pains of her labor
Were over and done
She looked into the face
Of God's precious Son

They placed Him in a manger
Where the animals were fed
This is where Jesus
First lay His head

The manger should have been called
A treasure chest
For by the baby it held
The world has truly been blessed

As Jesus the Savior

Grew into a man

He was fulfilling

God's master plan


Jesus is the greatest gift

This world has ever known

For He provides us a way

To the Heavenly throne

# JESUS PAID THE PRICE

We were all guilty
But Jesus paid the cost
He gave His life
For the souls that were lost

Our sins were so great
No other sacrifice would suffice
Jesus gave His precious life
He paid the price

The world was filled with
Wickedness and sin
There was no place
For hope to begin

God looked down
And saw a world filled with pain
So He gave us Jesus
The Lamb that was slain

We were guilty of sin
But Jesus stood trial
The people that were there
Were in denial

That this indeed
Was God's precious only Son
Someone had to pay for our sins
And Jesus was the one


Jesus was mocked
Tormented and whipped
They beat Him so bad
That His skin became ripped


He could have called angels
To lift the burden from Him
But Jesus did not want
Our life to be grim


Jesus looked through time
And saw us in our sin
He knew that when death took us
Our time in Hell would begin


The thought of our suffering
Brought tears to His eyes
So He took our place
He gave His life


Jesus suffered a death

Filled with pain

He was God's precious Son

The Lamb that was slain


Accept Jesus as your Savior

This is my advice

Jesus died for all of us

He paid the price

# SWEET JESUS

My sweet Jesus
I'm so glad to earth you came
Since you entered my life
It has never been the same

You gave me joy
And such sweet peace
My love for You
Continues to increase

You have seen me through the good times
You have seen me through the bad
You have been with me when I'm happy
You have been with me when I'm sad

Sweet Jesus there have been times
I felt I could not go on
You picked me up and carried me
Through the darkness and the dawn

Jesus you have been there
To calm my deepest fears
You have also been there
To dry my flowing tears

Jesus without You my soul

Would forever be lost

I am so glad I trusted You

For my sins You paid the cost


You were hanged on a cross

On Calvary's hill

And from Your side

Your blood did spill


That precious blood

Washed away my sin

When I opened my heart

And let You in


They placed You in a tomb

On that sad day

But in the tomb

You did not stay


Your were held by death

But you broke the ties

Then from the tomb

You did rise


The victory over death

You did achieve
Now forever to You
I will cleave

Until I see you
In Heaven so fair
Then I will bow at your feet
And worship you there

# GIFT FROM JESUS

When I was saved
By God's amazing grace
The misery in my heart
Christ's love did replace

When I accepted the gift of Salvation
I took on a new role
Jesus gave peace
To my poor troubled soul

I could never have bought
This wonderful gift
If it were not for Jesus
I would be adrift

I received this gift
Free and without cost
When I accepted Jesus
My soul was no longer lost

Jesus entered my heart
And forgave my sin
I felt no despair
Only peace within

There are times I am happy
And I have a smile
My Savior Jesus
Made my life worthwhile

There are times I am sad
And the tears may flow
I have a place
I know I can go

I get on my knees
And talk to Jesus in prayer
Happy or sad
He is always there

Jesus guides me
As I go along my way
He will come
To get me someday

Then this wicked world
I will no longer roam
Jesus will then take me
To my beautiful new home

I will be living

In glorious Heaven above

Surrounded by beauty

Harmony and love


I will be experiencing the wonders

Of the gift that Jesus gave

Because when I let Him in my heart

My soul He did save

# JESUS QUIETS A STORM

Jesus and His disciples
Entered a ship
For the disciples this would be
An amazing trip

Jesus went to sleep
He needed to rest
Soon His disciples
Would be very stressed

A raging storm started
After they had set sail
The disciples became worried
That they would not prevail

The wind blew hard
And the waves rose high
The disciples were sure
They were going to die

The ship was tossed
As the water spilled in
The disciples were filled
By fear from within

The disciples were scared
And consumed by dread
They felt that surely soon
They would all be dead

The disciples went to Jesus
So He they could awake
They felt for sure
Their lives were at stake

Jesus loved His disciples
And they He did cherish
They awoke Him saying
"Lord save us we perish"

Jesus arose from His rest
Then went to face the storm
He was getting ready
Another miracle to perform

Jesus looked at waves
And said "Peace be still"
The wind and waves ceased
His will to fulfill

The disciples then marveled

About Jesus that very day
What manner of man is this
That the wind and waves do obey

The disciples learned
When danger does impend
Jesus will be there for you
He is your greatest friend

# FRUIT OF THE SPIRIT

When we are saved
By God's loving grace
We should always have
A smile on our face

The fruit of the Spirit
We should always show
As we walk along life's pathway
As onward we go

One of the fruits is a
Generous sweet love
It is sent to us
By God up above

Another of the fruits
Is glorious joy
Our salvation through Jesus
The Devil can't destroy

We are also given
A deep restful peace
The gladness in our heart
Will surely increase

With the fruit of longsuffering
We can surely endure
For Jesus washed away our sins
And made our souls pure

In our life each day
We can show the fruit of gentleness
If we do this
God surely will bless

With the fruit of goodness
We can having a caring heart
Thanks to the blood of Jesus
From God we will not depart

With the fruit of faith
We will not doubt
We should share with others
What Jesus is all about

With the fruit of meekness
We can be patient and kind
When Jesus comes again
We will not be left behind

With the fruit of temperance

We can show restraint
To do God's work
We should never say I can't

These fruits are gifts given
By the Father above
We should tell others
About His wonderful love

So of these fruits
They to can share
And one day we can all meet
In Heaven so fair

# Alphabetical Index of Poems

# COLOPHON

Reflections of the Soul Christian Poetry Book Three in the Heart and Soul Christian Poetry Collection is independently published.